CH00958545

This Blue Mantle

Jenny Vuglar

Hearing Eye

HEARING EYE
TORRIANO MEETING HOUSE
POETRY PAMPHLET SERIES No. 46

Hearing Eye
Box 1, 99 Torriano Avenue
London NW5 2RX, UK
email: books@hearingeye.org
www.hearingeye.org
www.torriano.org

Poems © Jenny Vuglar 2006
ISBN: 1-905082-22-3

Acknowledgements
Some of these poems have appeared in the following publications: *Acumen,
Ambit, Landfall* (NZ), *Magma, Mother Earth Journal* (USA), *Poetry NZ, Second
Light Newsletter, Staple, The Interpreter's House, The SHOp, The Rialto* and
Westwords magazines; and *In the Company of Poets* anthology (Hearing Eye).

This publication has been made possible with
the financial support of Arts Council England

Printed by Catford Print Centre

Designed by Martin Parker

Cover image: 'Abstract Picture – Blue; after Richter' by Martin Parker

Contents

The House among the Marshes

Between the north field, with its long roll of stubble,
and the sand rising to a bar, salt marshes sink and shimmer.
Birds call, dip at the house, descend.

This is not summer: clouds bank and hover,
the sand is pock-marked with rain.
It is the year's end and all this green
someone else's bright day and long evening.

The water fills with returning cries,
a runway of birds, feet first, plummeting:
the geese heavy, the water silver.

I could live here, in the house among the marshes,
watch birds land, listen to reeds rasp like paper knives,
see water sparkle and preen; be still,
while the sky moved around me, full of wings
calling, flinging light from water to reed's blade,
from the swan's black beak to the feathers
that dance and wave on her back; sleep,
while the dark settled like silt in the reeds and the sea
murmured beyond the bar.

And if I slept here, in the house among the marshes,
nothing would wake me but the rushing of wings.

Covehithe, January

Listen, the woodpecker taps out a rapid staccato,
there are gunshots somewhere, one or two, then silence.
My last words melt, disappear in a puff of white.
The trees pick their black way home across fields fresh
ploughed, white with the year's christening.

Someone has cracked the ice, cracked and lifted it
in thick shards, from the pigs' trough.
They look up, one stands nose lifted into the wind
as snow begins, snow rushing out of a blue sky,
like light, like the melt-water of stars.

Beyond Blue

There is no night, but in this winter sun
a bat is flickering, between trees, into the clearing
and out again. A small hole in this blue.
There is a sound like the rushing of souls,
too many to count, all passing on one breath.
They turn, the white vapour of their sighing
breaks the sky open.

It is this blue mantle, his mother's apron that she folds
and refolds. Where the ember landed there is one small hole.
There is no darning it, she holds it up to the light.

There are two bats up among the angels,
moving as the music moves, the violin's staccato,
beating time. Around and around
they fly until everyone is watching, breathless:
a church full of upturned faces.

The great wings of angels spread out;
splinters float down like feathers, bolts creak.
When the music is over, they will be gone –
there will be a great noise of wings and the roof
will lift. The whole sky will fall in.

Winter's Day

If I had long fingers
they could reach the earth beneath ice
this winter's day.

Nothing is moving.

Not even wind can stir
these stiffened relicts,
the skeleton trees, the sharpened yew.
Topiary makes angles like prisms
breaking the light into every shade of grey.

Listen, the earth rings under our feet.
There is no softness.

The children walk across the pond.
Below today's ice, yesterday's thickens,
sweet reed-grass withers,
pellets of ice shift in the wind.

They are the only birds singing
their frozen voices crack the grey sky.

White Horses

Our horse won the Avondale Cup one year,
from behind, coming up on the outside.

All winter the record played, the commentator's
excitement lifted us high each time.

Even my sister learnt to place the needle carefully
to hit just the right spot. They were off.

Uncle Jack drank whiskey in the bathroom before breakfast.
It was the cold. Getting up at six to work the horses.

Fog made everything invisible until you got up close.
The rails around the horse paddocks would suddenly appear,
dark and solid; then disappear.

The horses were led out tossing their heads like Pegasus.
Even gelded they stropped about, oat-fed, skipping
sideways when the rails did their looming trick.

The jockeys were my height but iron-hard.
They moved like cats, even their eyes thinned.

I sat on rails watching them thunder in and out of fog,
shadows wreathed in steam, eyes rolled on victory,

clutching the white horses off the whiskey bottle
so hard the marks stayed on my palms forever.

Northland

New Zealand 9 July 1962

The last beach, pointing North,
the thin strip of land we stood upon.

The oceans were always too close for comfort.

At night I could hear the crash of seas,
where the spirits leap, see the sky open.

On a globe I traced the outline with my finger
so narrow a thick pen would obliterate us;

if I looked up, the sky was the same blue.
It was everywhere, we were drifting in it.

Rata and I crept into the porch to play knuckle bones.
We were hidden there, the light was oblique.
We played all afternoon, the same game, over and over.
Inside we could hear singing.

The day was so long we hid, crawled under the house,
hearts thumping against the floorboards.
The music here was muffled by feet tapping,
light shone thinly between the cracks.

We lay in the dust until we heard them calling,
came out and the sky was crimson red.

When I went home no one scolded. I bathed
and ate and watched the bone white stars go out.
'The sea is burning', I said and no one spoke
but all night the sky grew redder till I slept.

I dreamt of water flaming in the air,
of sea like lava, of everything there was afire.

But in the morning all there was, was blue.

*9 July 1962 was the day of the American 'airburst' nuclear test over
Johnston's Atoll. The red afterglow was visible from the far north of New Zealand
where I observed it as a child.*

The Sheep

Pain kept you awake,
afterwards you wondered if
by some freak of wind you'd heard.

The dogs killed silently
or water did, the weight of wool
pulling them under.
Those that lived long enough for you to kill
lay deep in culverts
their flanks ribboned.

I stopped the words that welled like blood in your throat,
could not bear spoken this that lay upon our tongues.

Sacking holds the sheep,
skinned and gutted, heads and feet gone.
The waste of everything
lies between us.

Bending the carcass
you chop where tendons bind bone to bone.
The sheep dismembers neatly.

Finished, you wipe your hands on the apron.
The fat gleams, blood makes sequins on it.

In My Father's Conservatory

This is a room that is here and not here,
attached, but oh so distant:
part of the sky.
Clouds move through it, whispering
of mountains, the rug rucks up
in small peaks, the tips bleach white.

This is the room we long for, stretch
out for, sun stripped, the glass table burning.
At night wind slaps against the glass,
trees move, tall and dark,
possums rustle, the orchids
hanging in chains, swing.

The sun sleeps, curled about us,
the moon rises and falls.
Newspapers spread out, unseen,
the tea grows cold.
This morning a fantail flew in,
passing between us, sudden, swift.

A rushing of wings, a cloud.
And you – you with your head back
watching the stars fall,
socks on your feet, thick as slippers,
a cigarette shadowing your fingers –
you are listening.

The bird is still singing.

Whangamata Road, New Zealand

that's a good job of breaking in
he said
pointing from the road
to a jagged bone bare slope
rising steep as the new moon
out of the dark bush sky

you wouldn't believe it
would you
he said
what good land can be broken
from these rubbishy hills
it's a crying shame
the way it's left to rot

leaf mould under fallen stump
silence creeping like algae
in the valleys

a few more roads like this'll
see it opened up

sheep clinging like astronauts
to its broken face
grass like gauze
embalming bone

the road we travel
like a sliced up wrist
bleeding the land dry

The Pirate Ship

(from a photograph of Childwall Valley Children's Playground)

A burnt out ship shoulders the mist.
The trees are limbless, the dark has swept in
like a vicious surgeon.

The iron bars of civic seats are plankless,
the tree trunks graduation charred;
out of the asphalt white grass is shrivelling
under a bitch's piss.

Into all this strides someone I used to know,
hair to his shoulders, black and thick,
boots buckled, the waistcoat and jacket stiff
with last year's fear.

He can't believe they've done this to him,
burnt his ship, left him landlocked
in all this waste. The mist rolls in,
he holds it in his fingers.

The boys shiver, pass a stolen cigarette
between cupped hands. They're tired of him,
his posturing, his endless talk
of flying out of here,

want to be just the lost boys again.
To do nothing but sit in this cold December day
and watch, through blackened timbers,
how the mist rolls in.

Letter to Paul (1)

People die every day. The boy on the poster at yesterday's march –
his uncle was it? or just a stranger, carrying his death above us.
I was a pall bearer for a moment, I and those around who glanced up.
'My nephew,' it said, 'killed by US imperialism.'
He wasn't the first, people are disappearing one after another
– my father's football team for example. All gone, he says.

I remember you standing in the black of a pub garden,
the thin tip of your cigarette shining. I'd said 'Go out,
I can't breathe.' My father blowing smoke out the car window,
tapping ash into the wind. The smell of the match, that quick
flare of memory. I'd wanted a moment alone.
'It's fine,' you said in your rough voice, 'I'm fine.'

You anticipate me now, say 'I know there's nothing to say'
and there isn't. We laugh. What did we laugh about?
I can't remember. It seems absurd, the planes are still flying
their ridiculous missions – sometimes they fly so low I swear
they know I'm here, cocking a snook at my useless cursing.
The birds shake themselves down.

This afternoon, like Whitman, I chopped wood or rather
(because I want to be honest) cut with a long bow saw,
one foot up on a chair, steadying branches broken from an oak.
Last winter's storm. It makes me feel virtuous, virtuous and
connected. Part of the day as the leaves on the beech
are part of it, and the birds, huddled, out of reach.

I know this backwoods libertarianism is romantic and that
the world continues on as shittily as ever despite my storing carbons
and dreaming of disconnecting from the grid – but it feels right
to use my arms and afterwards to walk out across fields
where next year's over-production of wheat is pushing through
and the beet mountain is growing on its concrete slab.

There are three men working on the church, up on ladders
painting the gutters and downpipes. They let me in to
the usually locked tower where the whitewashed banner
closet is full of mops and brooms. I stand in the middle so the
four foot Saxon walls surround me and I know it's crazy but I feel
part of time – still temporal but so long it doesn't matter.

I can cope with a thousand years, it's this absurd shortening
of breath, the cutting-off of life for no reason –
a boy falling with a milk bottle in his hand, a shadow on an X-ray,
these planes with their howl of death that reach across into
unimagined lives – this boy who is as we will be.
People die every day. Don't.

Letter to Paul (2)

This time of year it's easy to be in love with life – there it comes
rushing out of the ground, green so vivid it hurts. That bright
your eyes still narrowed against even after nearly thirty years in
this quiet light. I never heard a single reminiscence that wasn't people
but there it was, the landscape written in your skin, the way
you put a hand up to shade your eyes, in the pub garden,
at lunchtime, even in winter.

You moved house and I designed a garden for you – wide borders
of grand gestures: dramatic, intense. You never built any of it.
I hadn't left room for Toby's bonfire night, for barbecues,
for all those who trekked up the stairs to our top floor office,
warning letters in their hands. Once I took a calculator
and tried to work out just how much the team budget
should have for shop steward activities.

You told me not to be so bloody stupid. 'Never give the other side
ammunition,' you said. You never did your timesheets.
Sounds prophetic now doesn't it? You didn't want to know.
Even last week you kept wandering back to the moment
they told you. Still shocked. Still trying to process it.
Now, looking at all that green leaping out of the ground,
so am I. I can't take it in. I can't think of anything.

Last night I got drunk and wept and remembered you
driving me home after too many whiskies and telling
me about saxophones and circular breathing and how
it fooled breathalysers – and then the time you drove Linda
and me back from France, weaving across lanes, knocking
against the central reservation on the motorway.
God knows how you survived this long.

But that's what I loved. You weren't careful, you didn't
plot life out or watch your back. You just went on,
a bloody minded Australian still singing the *Internationale*
even after the Berlin Wall came down. So in a way
I'm glad it's May – May Day and all that solidarity – and then the
first real sun of the year, as though you're looking over my shoulder,
as though that abundance you had has spilled over into everything,

all this tumbling growth, all these new leaves,
all this green.

The Underwriter from Lloyds

I can feel the rain coming, the way
the wind lifts, the way the poplars whiten.

I can hold a boat upright in a storm;
twist sails in and out of wind.

I can hold four glasses and not spill a drop
though the walls close and the floor rocks.

I can see numbers like small lights
in the dark, green or the white of street lamps.

I can plot the course of a wave,
watch the wind swirl without missing an equation.

I can stand anywhere, and with nothing but
fingertips, feel the rain coming.

In Time

There was a day when I saw how,
in time, the dead would blacken the sky —
uncalled except by the stirring of a drink
or today, biting into a ciabatta
the light dusting of flour on my lips
tasting like skin.

And more than that, how even
the unnoticed transits we make through this city
become afterwards, journeys;
the street names white in the headlights:
Jerningham, Vesta, Waller. Street after street crossed
until the river winds around a boneyard.

The sky is full of men on ladders
placing silver against silver,
building a long curve
that settles over the roof tops like a rainbow.
Promises, promises. When I am old
my eyelids will droop under the weight.

Arch Triumphant

I am arrested, as I often am,
held between doing and not,
eavesdropping on something known already —

sweeping petals off the table
my curled fist cupped around nothing
fragments already gone
sloughed off
                my own skin
held between two hands like dust

or watching the dark come in
the stiff black of the acacia waiting for wind —
turning, the creak and groan of my back
like a wave of sorrow for something happened.

The lights that must go out;
the arch triumphant over the Oval
already black.

Beethoven's Death Mask

Beethoven's death mask hums
when the sun falls on it, it sings –
not loud, a contented bass
looking up at the sky and twisting
those long-gone arms back –
a pillow to lie upon.

So quiet today he might be sleeping,
that thick impassive skin.
It's not deafness he complains of
but lack of sight.
Blank swollen lids tap their way around the room.
Undressing in front of him was never a problem.

The best times are afternoons when
the stillness is companionable, not awkward;
when the sun picks out
every ripple
every time-etched pock-mark.
He hums, I sit on the bed –
it's all blue, nothing to ground us.
Sonatas, concertos – all under his breath.
I listen.
The black print dances.

write / contribute   Greyscapes

picturing it for becoming whimsical

I'd ihave to tackle the big ones
            Sottojit & Paul poems

        ...... Broth Nich
    ...'a preserve qte dead ..... Cruz.

Grotesques
        ... ... death